This is a Dorling Kindersley Book
published by Random House, Inc.

Editors Andrea Pinnington, Charlotte Davies
Designer Heather Blackham
Managing Editor Jane Yorke
Senior Art Editor Mark Richards
Photography Steve Gorton
Series Consultant Neil Morris

First American edition, 1991

Library of Congress Cataloging-in-Publication Data
My first look at things that go.
p. cm.
Originally published by Dorling Kindersley Ltd., London.
Summary: Text and photographs depict various forms of
transportation, such as boats, trucks, planes, and spaceships.
ISBN 0-679-81804-9
1. Vehicles – Juvenile literature. [1. Vehicles.] I. Random
House (Firm)
TL147.M9 1991
629.04 - dc20
90-23562

Manufactured in Italy 1 2 3 4 5 6 7 8 9 10

Reproduced by Bright Arts, Hong Kong
Printed in Italy by L.E.G.O.

· MY · FIRST · LOOK · AT ·

Things that go

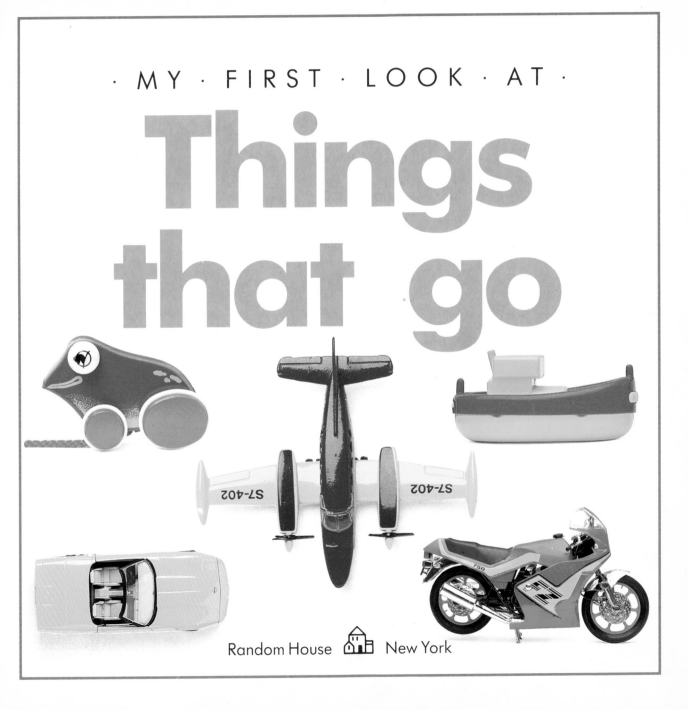

Random House 🏠 New York

On the road

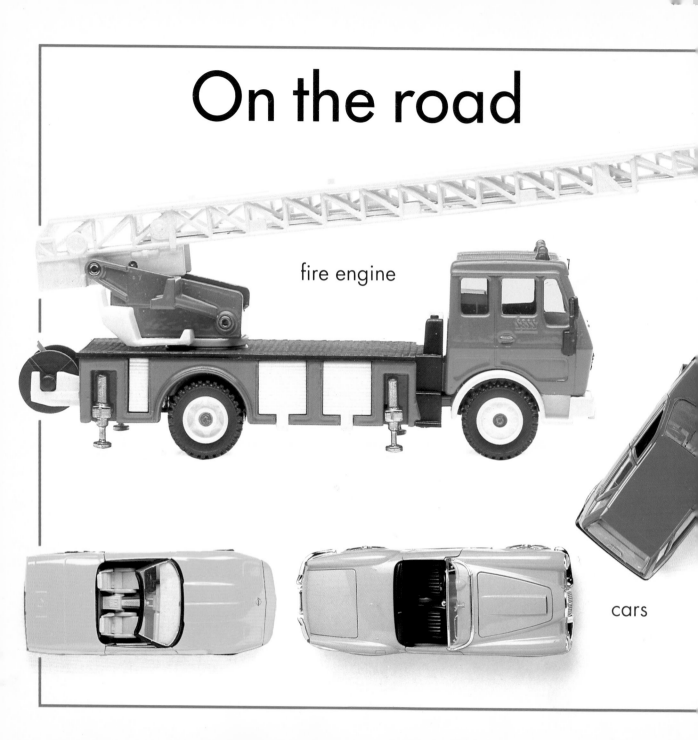

fire engine

cars

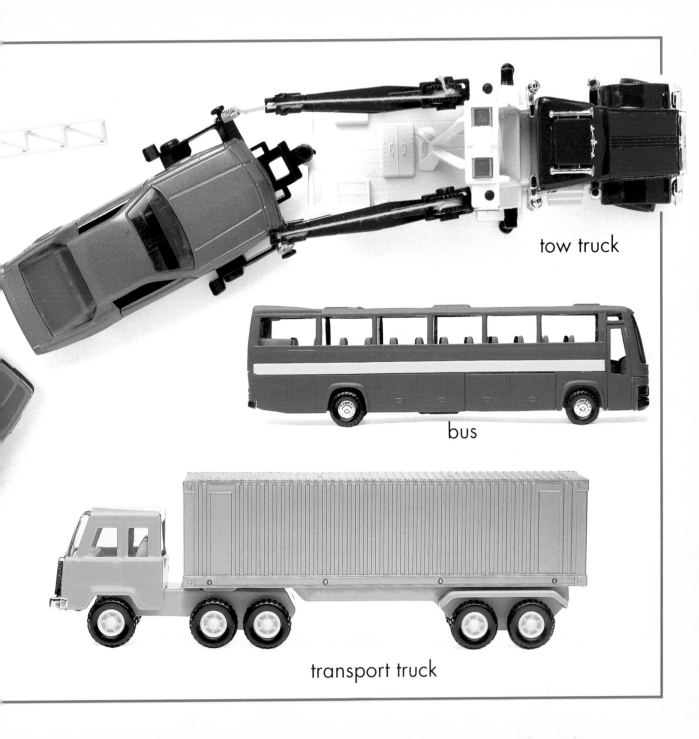

tow truck

bus

transport truck

Toys that go

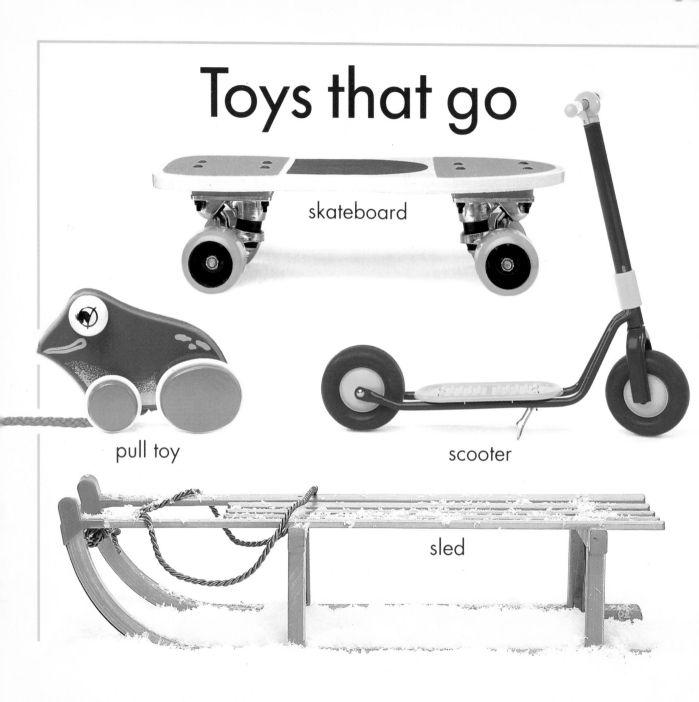

skateboard

pull toy

scooter

sled

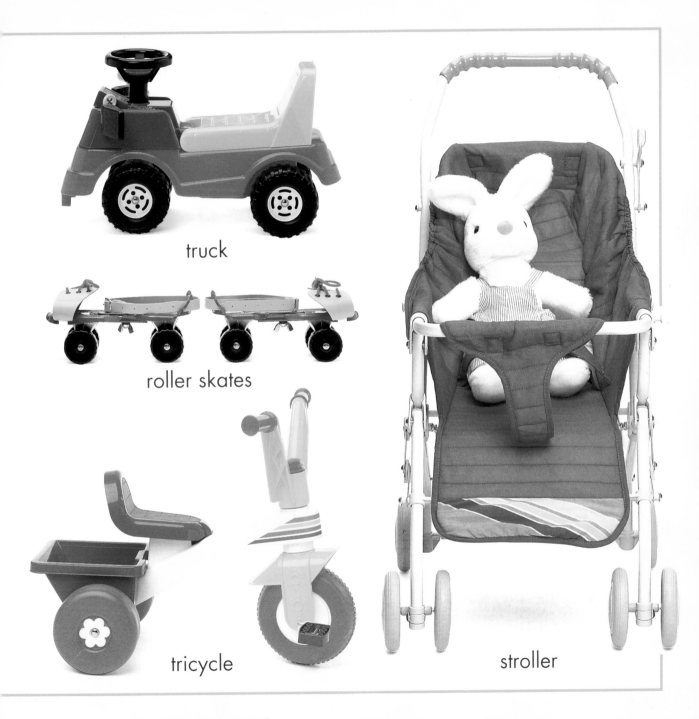

truck

roller skates

tricycle

stroller

On tracks

steam engine

freight cars

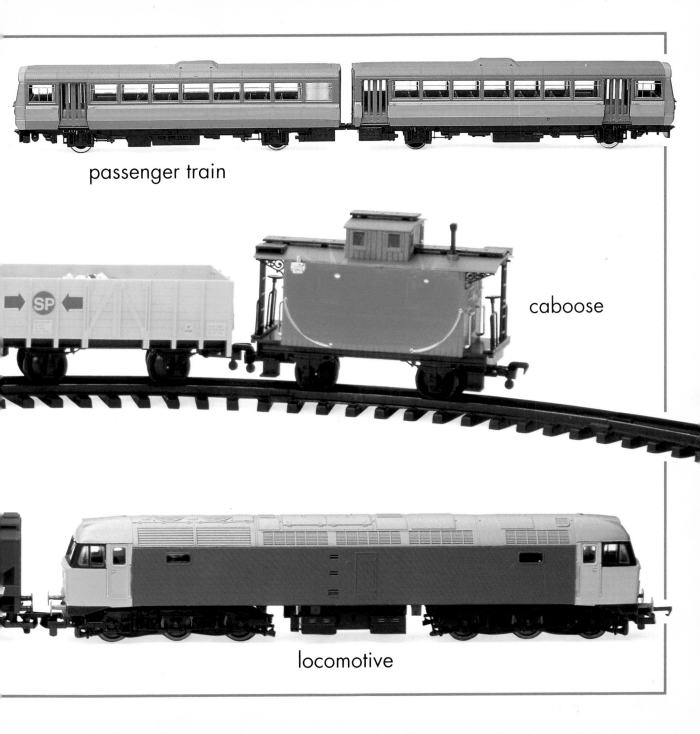

passenger train

caboose

locomotive

On the building site

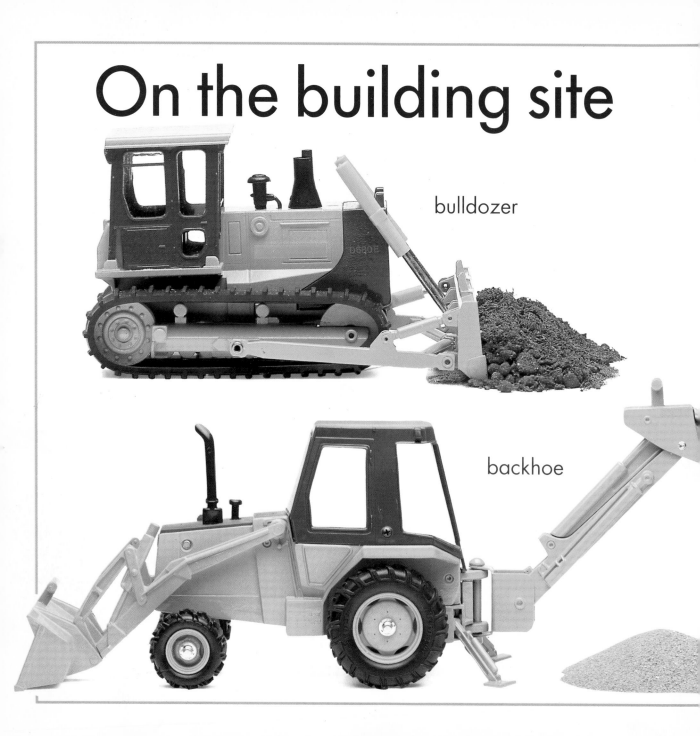

bulldozer

backhoe

cement mixer

dump truck

On the farm

jeep and horse trailer

tractor

trailer

combine
harvester

plow

In the air

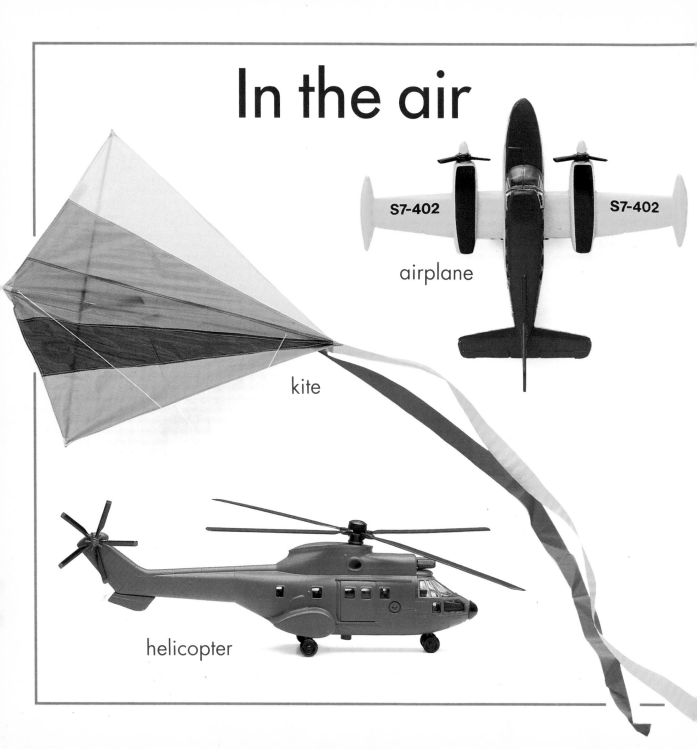

airplane

kite

helicopter

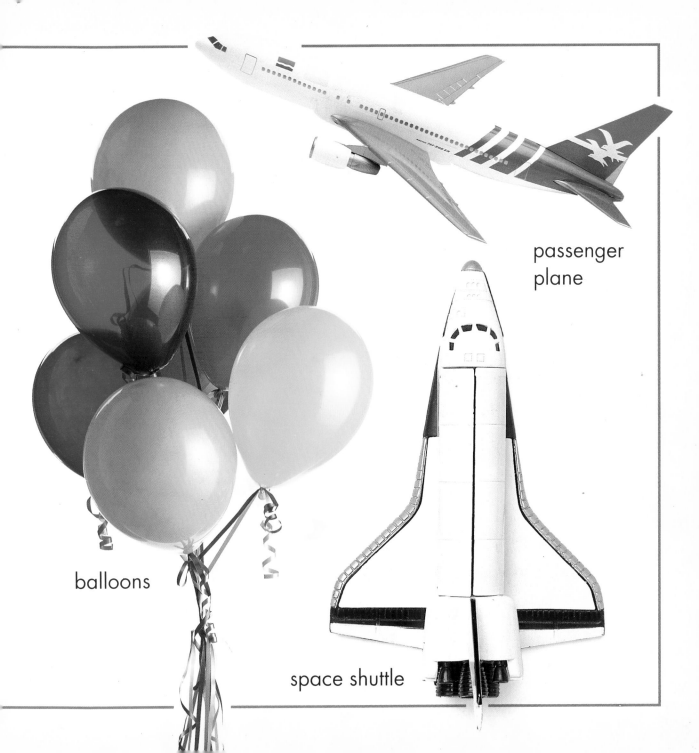

passenger
plane

balloons

space shuttle

In the water

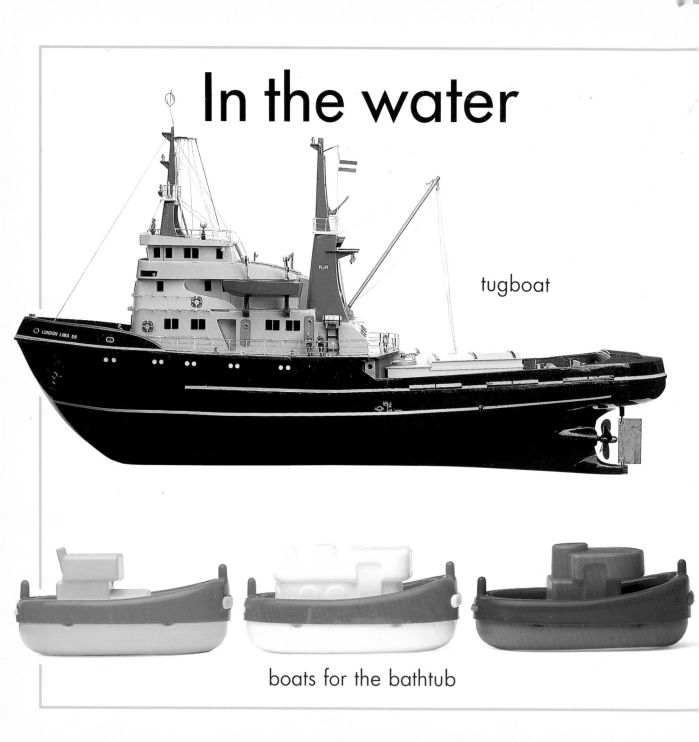

tugboat

boats for the bathtub

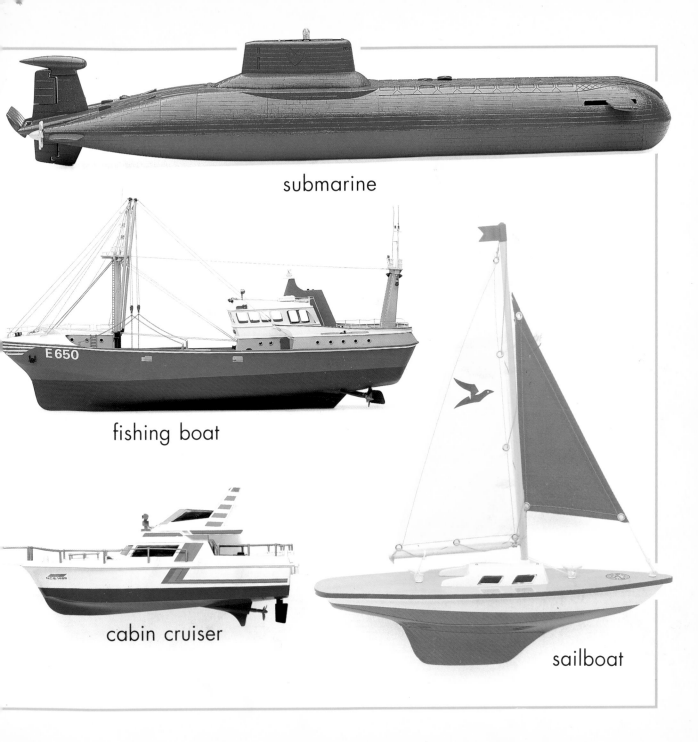

submarine

fishing boat

E 650

cabin cruiser

sailboat

Things that go fast

speedboat

racing car

motorcycle

Things that go slow

traction engine

steamroller

glider